East Africa

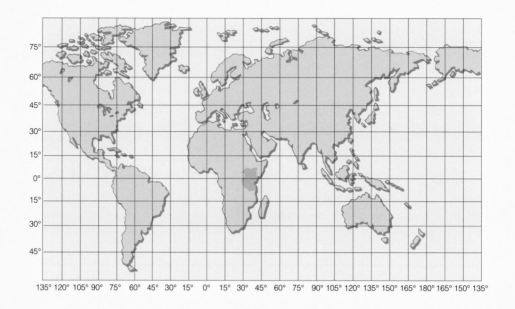

EAST AFRICA

country	area (sq mi)	population (1995)	capital	currency
KENYA	244,980	28,300,000	Nairobi	Kenyan Shilling (KSh) = 100 cents
TANZANIA	364,930	29,700,000	Dar es Salaam	Tanzanian Shilling (TSh) = 100 cents
UGANDA	91,140	21,300,000	Kampala	New Ugandan Shilling (NUSh) = 100 cents

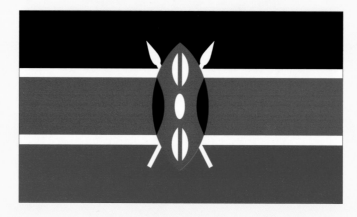

Kenya

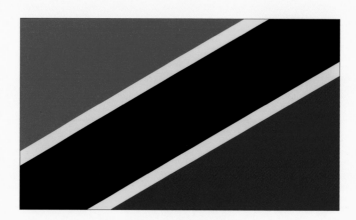

Tanzania

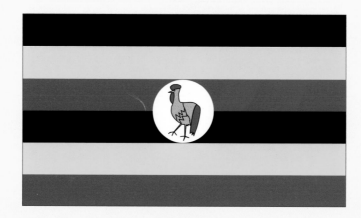

Uganda

East Africa

Rob Bowden
and Tony Binns

RSVP

RAINTREE
STECK-VAUGHN
P U B L I S H E R S
The Steck-Vaughn Company

Austin, Texas

Published by Raintree Steck-Vaughn Publishers, an imprint of Steck-Vaughn Company

Design and typesetting	Roger Kohn Designs
Commissioning editor	Hazel Songhurst
Editor	Merle Thompson
Assistant editor	Diana Russell
Picture research	Paula Chapman
Maps	János Márffy

We are grateful to the following for permission to reproduce photographs:
Front Cover: Panos *above* (Sean Sprague); Getty Images *below* (Daryl Balfour); Axiom, pages 9 (Jim Holmes), 17 (Jim Holmes), 25 (Jim Holmes), 45 *right* (Jim Holmes); Tony Binns, pages 18 *above* and *below*, 19 a*bove*, 24 *below*, 33; B Coleman, pages 16 (Paul van Gaalen), 36 (Andy Purcell), 40 a*bove* (Christer Fredriksson); Eye Ubiquitous, page 43 *above* (Thelma Sanders); Getty Images, pages 10 (Rene Lynn), 12 (Nicholas Parfitt); Robert Harding, pages 8 *below*, 11 (N A Callow), 31; Hutchinson, pages 13 *below* (Patricio Goycolea), 41 (Crispin Hughes); Images of Africa, pages 8 *above* (David Keith Jones), 15 (David Keith Jones), 28 (David Keith Jones), 29 (Peter Tilbury), 39 *above* (David Keith Jones); Impact, pages 13 *above* (Javed A Jafferji), 14 (Javed A Jafferji), 30 *above* (Javed A Jafferji), 30 *below* (Piers Cavendish), 34 (Jorn Stjerneklar), 35 (Caroline Penn), 37 *above* and *below* (Piers Cavendish), 40 *below*; Panos, pages 20 (Betty Press), 21 (Sean Sprague), 23 (Jeremy Hartley), 24 *above* (S Hackett), 32 (Trygve Bølstad), 39 *below* (Sean Sprague), 43 *below*, (Sean Sprague), 44 (Crispin Hughes), 45 *left* (Liba Taylor); Popperfoto, page 27; WPL, pages 22, 38.

The statistics given in this book are the most up-to-date available at the time of going to press.

Printed in Hong Kong by Wing King Tong

Library of Congress Cataloging-in-Publication Data
Binns, Tony.
East Africa / Tony Binns and Rob Bowden.
p.   cm. — (Country fact files)
Includes bibliographical references and index.
Summary: Introduces the landscape, climate, natural resources, people, and culture of the countries of East Africa.
ISBN 0-8172-5401-3 (alk. paper)
1. Africa, East — Juvenile literature.   [1. Africa, East.]
I. Bowden, Rob.   II. Title.   III. Series.
DT423.B56   1998
967 — dc21   97-40221
                                          CIP   AC

1 2 3 4 5 6 7 8 9 0 WK 01 00 99 98 97

CONTENTS

Words that are explained in the glossary are printed in
SMALL CAPITALS the first time they are mentioned in the text.

INTRODUCTION

East Africa consists of three countries – Kenya, Tanzania, and Uganda. It covers a total area of 681,049 square miles (1,763,780 sq km), making it seven times bigger than the U.K. and almost one-fifth the size of the U.S. In 1995 the region's population was nearly 80 million. Added to various African ethnic groups, this included people of European, Arabic, and Asian origin; a legacy of the area's colonial past. East Africa has a very long history of human settlement. It has often been called "The Cradle of Humankind," since the world's most ancient human remains have been found here.

The Great Rift Valley dominates East Africa and incorporates many spectacular features, such as Lake Victoria, the mountains of Kilimanjaro and Mount Kenya, and the SODA LAKES Nakuru and Natron, with their masses of pink flamingoes. Wildlife is abundant throughout much of the region, and vast areas of land are dominated by millions of wildebeest, zebra, and antelope.

Nairobi, Mombasa, Dar es Salaam, and Kampala are thriving modern cities in stark contrast to the vast SAVANNA plains of Tanzania, the rain forests of western Uganda, and the remote deserts of northern Kenya. These cities reflect East Africa's relatively advanced development compared with other African countries. Still the region is very poor. Many rural people, such as NOMADIC Turkana, face a daily struggle to survive.

▼ *Nairobi, seen here from across Uhuru (Freedom) Park, is East Africa's biggest city and one of the most important cities on the African continent.*

East Africa can be summarized as an area full of variety. Within its three countries, you will find almost anything you might imagine about the continent of Africa as a whole. This book explores this region, looking at its people, places, and policies, and suggesting what its future direction and opportunities may be.

EAST AFRICA AT A GLANCE

- Area: 682,485 square miles
- Population (1995): 79.3 million
- Population density: Average of 116.5 people per square mi (80 per square mi in Tanzania; 127 in Kenya; 233 in Uganda)
- Capital cities: Dar es Salaam (Tanzania); Kampala (Uganda); Nairobi (Kenya)
- Other main cities: Nairobi 1,500,000; Dar es Salaam 1,360,000; Kampala 773,000; Mombasa 465,000
- Highest mountain: Kilimanjaro (Tanzania), 19,340 feet
- Largest lake: Victoria, 26,835 square feet
- Languages: Swahili, English, African languages
- Major religions: Christianity, Islam, traditional African beliefs
- Life expectancy: 55 years (Kenya); 52 years (Tanzania); 44 years (Uganda)
- Currency: Kenyan shilling, written as $KSh ($KSh 1 = 100 cents); Tanzanian shilling, written as $TSh ($TSh 1 = 100 cents); New Ugandan shilling, written as $NUSh ($NUSh 1 = 100 cents)
- Economy: Mainly agricultural and services (chiefly tourism)

◀ *A Hindu temple in Kampala, Uganda, is evidence of the significant Asian population living in East Africa.*

THE LANDSCAPE

East Africa is bordered by a total of nine countries, including Mozambique, Rwanda, Congo, and Somalia. Uganda is landlocked, while Kenya and Tanzania both have an eastern coastline on the Indian Ocean. Tanzania's territory includes the small islands of Pemba and Zanzibar, which lie just off the coast.

The landscape in East Africa is dominated by the Great Rift Valley, an enormous GEOLOGICAL FAULT stretching 4,000 miles (6,400 km) from Jordan in the Middle East to Mozambique in southern Africa. The Rift Valley was created by massive earth movements over millions of years, twisting and buckling the surface to

▲ *Mount Kilimanjaro, the highest peak in Africa, rises impressively out of the scenic Amboseli National Park that surrounds it.*

cause some sections of land to rise and others to sink. The mountains, cliffs, valleys, and soda lakes that result from such movements can be found along the whole length of the fault, but those in East Africa provide some of the most impressive scenery in the world.

There are several mountains in East Africa, including Africa's highest, Mount Kilimanjaro (19,340 feet/5,895 m). It rises from the plains on the border of Kenya and

► *A tropical forest in Mount Kenya National Park.*

Tanzania, and its distinctive domed, snow-capped summit is visible from hundreds of miles away. Other peaks include Mount Kenya (17,057 ft/5,199 m), Mount Elgon (14,176 ft/4,321 m), and the Ruwenzori range in western Uganda (rising to 16,794 ft/5,119 m).

The Ruwenzori Mountains, also known as the "Mountains of the Moon" are particularly special because many rare plants and animals can be found in the tropical forests that cover their slopes. The forests extend westward across the border into Congo to form part of the massive Congo Basin, which covers more than 1.5 million square miles (4.1 million sq km) and includes the largest remaining area of tropical forest in Africa.

KEY FACTS

● Zanzibar is the largest coral island off the African coast, covering 637 square miles (1,650 sq km).

● At 26,835 square miles (69,500 sq km), Lake Victoria is the world's second largest freshwater lake after Lake Superior (31,815 sq mi/82,400 sq km) in the U.S./Canada.

● Ngorongoro, an extinct volcanic crater in northern Tanzania, is the second largest crater in the world.

Africa's largest lake, Lake Victoria, straddles the borders between Kenya, Tanzania, and Uganda. The lake is the starting point of the White Nile, which flows north through Uganda and into Sudan, joining the Blue Nile at Khartoum before flowing through Egypt to the Mediterranean. The region's other major rivers are the Tana and Galana in Kenya, and the Rufiji and Njombe in Tanzania, which all flow eastward to the Indian Ocean.

Other lakes in the region include Lake Turkana in northern Kenya, Lake Tanganyika on the Tanzania/Zaire border, and several soda lakes such as Lakes Nakuru and Bogoria in Kenya, and Lake

▲ *Savanna covers much of the East African landscape and is home to much of the region's abundant wildlife.*

Natron in Tanzania. These soda lakes have formed because the high temperatures in the region cause much of the water to evaporate, leaving behind salt deposits that make the water saltier than in normal lakes. Few animals can live in such salty water, but one bird that has adapted very well is the flamingo. Flamingos can be seen on the lakes in millions, especially at Lake Nakuru.

East Africa's 800 miles (1,300 km) of coastline are among the finest in the world. It includes an almost continuous belt of coral reefs that provide an important habitat for fish and other marine life. The white sand beaches and tropical vegetation also make the coast an attractive tourist area.

The vast expanses of savanna grassland that cover much of the rest of East Africa are home to many of the region's people and much of its rich wildlife. Areas of savanna such as the Serengeti and the Masai Mara contain some of the greatest concentrations of wildlife in the world. In northern Kenya the savanna turns into a SEMIARID landscape where few people live and very little grows.

▲ *The white sands and clear blue sea of Zanzibar's coast attract thousands of tourists annually.*

▶ *The edges of the Great Rift Valley form steep slopes like these, which are called "escarpments." The valley can be seen in the distance.*

CLIMATE AND WEATHER

The climate and weather in East Africa are as varied as its landscape. It is generally warm throughout the year, with average temperatures ranging from 50° to 104°F (10° to 40°C). The coastal strip and the low valley areas are normally the hottest parts of the region, while the highland plains (such as those around Nairobi) are noticeably cooler. The mountainous areas are also much cooler; several of the highest are snow-capped throughout the year, even though they are almost on the Equator. Mount Kilimanjaro is so cold at the top that it even has glaciers. By contrast, the northernmost sections of the region are extremely hot for much of the year — temperatures of 113°F (45°C) are common near Lake Turkana in northern Kenya.

Rainfall is the most important element in the local climate. It arrives in two distinct seasons — the main or "long" rains between March and May, and the secondary or "short" rains between October and December. At the peak of the rains in April, there are often violent storms and 12-16 inches (300–400 mm) of rain fall in a single month — about the same as Los Angeles's annual total. Life in East Africa depends on the rains; the

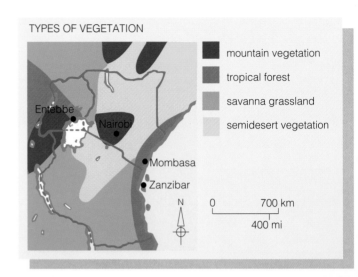

TYPES OF VEGETATION

- mountain vegetation
- tropical forest
- savanna grassland
- semidesert vegetation

Entebbe
Nairobi
Mombasa
Zanzibar

N   0   700 km
     400 mi

KEY FACTS

● Kampala, the Ugandan capital, has thunderstorms on more than 200 days in an average year.

● The region around Kericho in western Kenya has hailstorms on more than 100 days a year — one of the highest rates in the world.

● Tukuyu on Lake Malawi in Tanzania once recorded rainfall of 17 inches (432 mm) in a single day — more than normally falls in a month during the wet season.

▶ *During the rainy season, short and violent storms can often lead to serious flooding, as shown in this Zanzibar street. However, local people are used to this and know how to cope with it.*

amount that falls can mean the difference between life and death, both for the region's people and for its animals.

In the dry season, strong swirling winds create whirlwinds, or "dust devils," that can be seen racing across the plains, sometimes from hundreds of yards away. In the far north of Kenya, rainfall is so sparse that the people there have adopted a nomadic lifestyle. They may have to travel a long

▲ *Even though it stands just south of the Equator, the top of Mount Kilimanjaro is so cold that it has permanent glaciers.*

way on foot to find water and pasture for themselves and their animals. The extreme heat across much of East Africa means that water collected in lakes and rivers during the rains quickly evaporates. In some years even very large lakes can dry up completely.

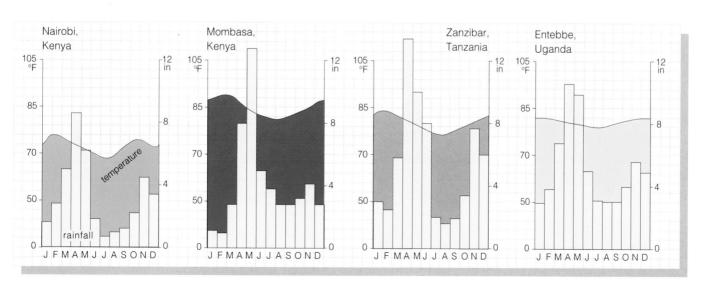

NATURAL RESOURCES

East Africa has relatively few natural resources compared with southern or western Africa, and very few compared with the U.S. and U.K. There are limited deposits of metals such as gold in Kenya and Tanzania, copper in Uganda, and tin in Tanzania, but nothing very significant in relation to world production figures. For example, Tanzania produced only 5.5 tons of tin in 1994, which places it below the top 20 world producers. Similarly, the region does have precious and semiprecious stones, including diamonds, rubies, and garnets, but nowhere near the quantity found in southern Africa.

East Africa's greatest resources are its land and wildlife. The land is intensively cultivated to produce CASH CROPS such as coffee, tea, cotton, and fruit and vegetable products, while the wildlife helps attract thousands of tourists, who bring valuable foreign currency to the region.

Most of the rural areas lack any form of electricity, so people meet their energy needs by collecting wood for burning. This can often take a long time and may involve walking great distances just to get enough to last for a few days. The process can also be damaging to the environment if wood is taken more quickly than the trees can replenish their numbers.

In the cities and towns, electricity is generated from imported oil or from hydro-

▼ *Wildlife is one of East Africa's key resources. It brings visitors from all over the world to places such as the Maasai Mara in Kenya.*

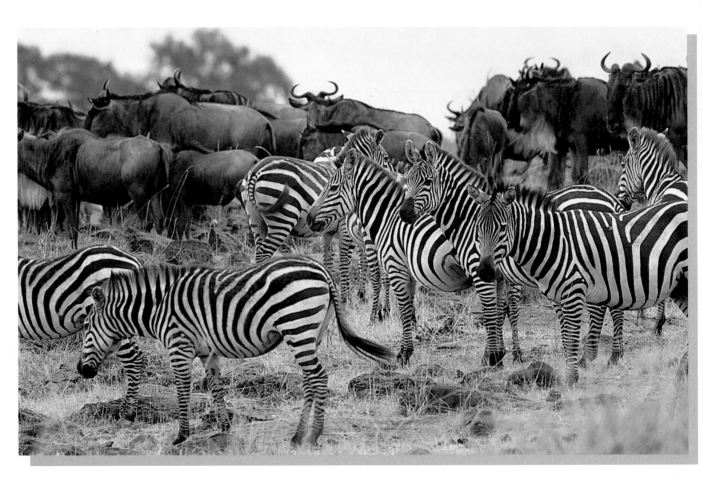

► *Firewood is a vital source of energy, and people may have to walk far to collect it. They carry it home on their heads. This is called "head-loading."*

KEY FACTS

● In 1994, Kenya produced less than 40 lbs. (20 kg) of gold, a tiny slice of total world production of more than 2,000 tons (2 million kg).

● 70–80% of the region's population rely on firewood for cooking, heating, and light.

● The Turkwel Gorge hydroelectric dam was built by the French in 1990. It now produces 105 megawatts of electricity a year: about 20% of Kenya's total needs in 1997.

● Kenya's Olkaria geothermal power plant, opened in 1981, produces 45 megawatts of electricity a year from three generators.

KEY NATURAL RESOURCES

KENYA	TANZANIA	UGANDA
gold	tin	copper
limestone	phosphates	cobalt
soda ash	iron ore	limestone
salt barites	coal	salt
rubies	diamonds	wildlife
fluorite	gemstones	
garnets	gold	
wildlife	natural gas	
	nickel	
	wildlife	

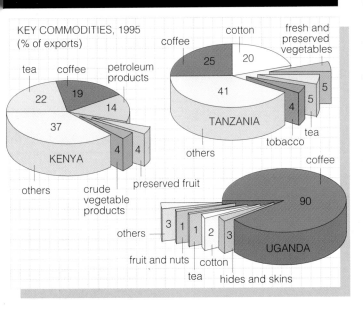

KEY COMMODITIES, 1995 (% of exports)

KENYA: tea 22, coffee 19, petroleum products 14, crude vegetable products 4, others 4, others 37

TANZANIA: coffee 25, cotton 20, fresh and preserved vegetables 5, tea 5, tobacco 4, others 41

UGANDA: coffee 90, cotton 3, tea 2, hides and skins 1, fruit and nuts 1, others 3, preserved fruit

electricity plants such as the Owen Falls Dam on Lake Victoria in Uganda and the Turkwel Gorge Dam in northern Kenya. A small amount of electricity is produced by using the heat of the volcanic earth at Olkaria, near Nakuru in central Kenya. This is a form of energy known as geothermal power. Some factories even produce electricity by burning crop waste. For example, a sugar-cane factory near Kakamega in western Kenya meets its electrical needs by burning the waste cane (bagasse) after the sugar has been squeezed from it.

POPULATION

The population of East Africa is among the fastest growing in the world, rising at an average of 3% per year. At this rate the region's 1995 population of 80 million will increase to reach more than 110 million in the year 2005, rising to nearly 200 million by 2025.

URBANIZATION

The cities are growing particularly fast, as overcrowding in rural areas forces people to move to urban centers in search of work. This process is called "rural–urban migration." The towns and cities cannot grow fast enough to cope with the migration, and around most large centers people have started building their own homes out of scrap materials. These "shantytowns" are often very crowded, with no fresh water or sanitation facilities. Some, like Mathare just outside Nairobi, are built in valleys, so that when the rains arrive they are often flooded, and people may lose all their possessions.

▲ *Like other large cities, Nairobi attracts people from the rural areas who hope to find jobs and homes.*

▼ *Shantytowns, such as this one in Mathare Valley outside Nairobi, have grown rapidly to house the large number of people who are moving into urban areas.*

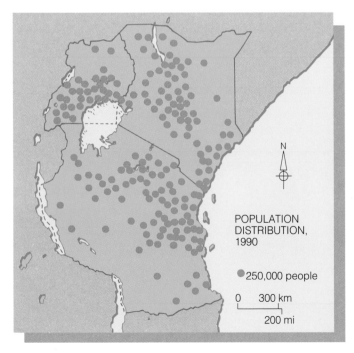

POPULATION DISTRIBUTION, 1990

● 250,000 people

0   300 km
    200 mi

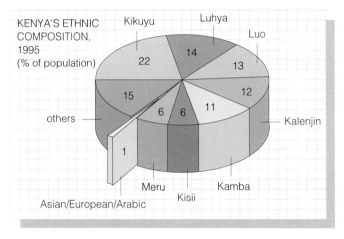

◀ *One of the smaller tribal groups, the Pokot people live in northwestern Kenya. These young women are in traditional dress to go to market.*

KENYA'S ETHNIC COMPOSITION, 1995 (% of population)

Kikuyu 22
Luhya 14
Luo 13
Kalenjin 12
11
6
6
others 15
1
Meru
Kisii
Kamba
Asian/European/Arabic

ETHNIC GROUPS

The vast majority of the population is African, but they are broken down into several different ethnic groups, or "tribes." In Kenya alone there are over 70 such groups, each with its own language and lifestyle. In the region as a whole, people can be split into two main groups: the Bantu and the Nilotic people. The Bantu are farmers, originally from western Africa, and include the Kikuyu in Kenya, the WaSukumu in Tanzania, and the Buganda in Uganda. The Nilotic people came from the Nile Valley area and are mainly PASTORALISTS. They include the Lango in Uganda, the Luo in Kenya, and the Masai, who live all over the region.

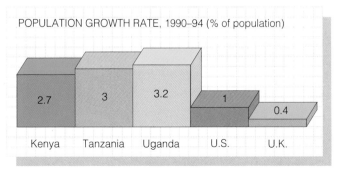

POPULATION GROWTH RATE, 1990–94 (% of population)

Kenya	Tanzania	Uganda	U.S.	U.K.
2.7	3	3.2	1	0.4

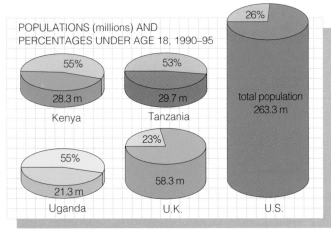

POPULATIONS (millions) AND
PERCENTAGES UNDER AGE 18, 1990–95

55%
28.3 m
Kenya

53%
29.7 m
Tanzania

55%
21.3 m
Uganda

23%
58.3 m
U.K.

26%
total population
263.3 m
U.S.

▲ *More than half the population of East Africa are children. Here in a Nairobi housing project, a group of boys are playing with toy cars and buses that they have made themselves out of scrap materials.*

MINORITY GROUPS

East Africa's history of colonial rule brought other groups to the region, too. Arabic people live along the coast, descendants of slave traders who once ruled that area. Their main city was Mombasa in Kenya, where the Arab influence can be seen in the architecture. The island of Zanzibar off the Tanzanian coast is still inhabited mainly by Arabic people.

Europeans colonized East Africa around 100 years ago, with the Germans ruling

Several of the tribal groups still fight each other over the ownership of traditional lands and animals, but these are normally small, local disputes rather than the major civil wars that neighboring African countries such as Congo and Mozambique have experienced in recent years.

KEY FACTS

● East Africa's population growth rate is 3 times faster than the U.S.'s and more than 7 times faster than the U.K.'s.

● In 1960, only 5% of Tanzania's population lived in towns and cities. In 1995, the figure was 24%.

● In 1950, 39% of Kenya's population was under the age of 14. By 1990, the figure had risen to 50%: the same as in Uganda and 1% more than in Tanzania.

● In 1995 there were more than 240,000 refugees in Kenya – about 200,000 of them from neighboring Somalia.

▶ **AIDS *is a major threat to East Africa's population. There are major efforts in all three countries to make people aware of the dangers of the disease.***

what is now Tanzania, and the British controlling Kenya and Uganda. After World War I, Tanzania also became British. Britain ruled the whole region until the early 1960s when it gained its INDEPENDENCE. Many Europeans still live in East Africa, either in the cities or on large farms and plantations. There are also many people of Asian descent in Kenya and Uganda whose ancestors arrived during British rule, mainly to work on the Mombasa–Uganda railroad. Kisumu, on the northeast shore of Lake Victoria, has a particularly high Asian population.

CURRENT ISSUES

Over 50% of East Africa's population is under 18 years old — more than double the proportion in most of Europe and North America. It is a challenge to provide schools, jobs, and homes for so many young people. And the rapidly growing population will continue to pose problems, as today's children marry and have children of their own.

One of the major problems facing the population today is AIDS. East Africa has one of the world's highest rates of HIV infection, (which leads to AIDS). The infection rate is especially high in urban areas. Governments and other organizations are working very hard to educate people about the dangers of AIDS, and posters reminding people of the risks can be seen throughout the region.

DAILY LIFE

Life is very hard for most of East Africa's people, who work long hours for little reward. Disease and malnutrition are also constant threats. Life expectancy has been slowly increasing over the past 20 years, but it is still only 55 years in Kenya and just 44 in Uganda — more than 30 years less than in the U.S. or U.K. and significantly less than in other developing countries such as India (62) or Brazil (67). Infant mortality is also high, with one in ten children in Tanzania and Uganda dying before their first birthday.

These figures are averages. The quality of people's daily lives is actually very different depending on whether they live in urban or rural areas.

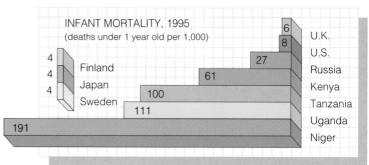

INFANT MORTALITY, 1995
(deaths under 1 year old per 1,000)

4	Finland
4	Japan
4	Sweden
6	U.K.
8	U.S.
27	Russia
61	Kenya
100	Tanzania
111	Uganda
191	Niger

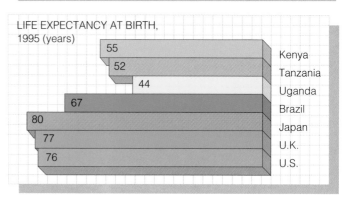

LIFE EXPECTANCY AT BIRTH, 1995 (years)

55	Kenya
52	Tanzania
44	Uganda
67	Brazil
80	Japan
77	U.K.
76	U.S.

◀ *For better-paid workers, such as this Asian family in Mombasa, Kenya, daily life is similar to that in western Europe or North America. Their apartment has fresh water, toilets, and electricity for lighting and modern appliances.*

URBAN LIFE

People in towns work in offices, banks, shops, factories, and restaurants much in the same way as people in North American cities. Many people also work in minimum wage jobs. Such jobs include polishing shoes, vending newspapers and magazines, washing windshields, selling fruit and vegetables on the street or in a market, and cleaning. With the urban population growing at about twice the national rate, minimum wage jobs are also expanding. If the

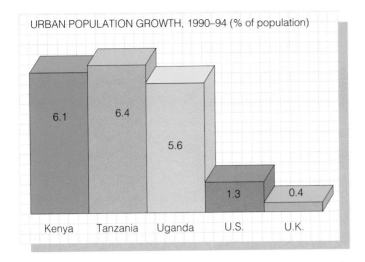

URBAN POPULATION GROWTH, 1990–94 (% of population)

Kenya	Tanzania	Uganda	U.S.	U.K.
6.1	6.4	5.6	1.3	0.4

population continues to increase so rapidly, unemployment in the urban areas is bound to increase.

Higher-paid workers live in apartments or in houses in the suburbs, but other workers live in shantytowns on the edge of urban areas or in villages some distance away, commuting into the center every day by public transportation. Few people earn enough to own a car. Instead, they rely on public buses or private minibuses or vans, known as MATATUS, that cover most of the main routes. Many of these vehicles overflow with passengers hanging out of the windows and doors.

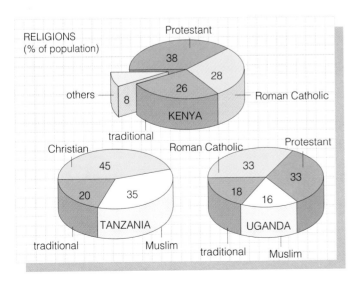

RELIGIONS
(% of population)

KENYA
- Protestant 38
- Roman Catholic 28
- traditional 26
- others 8

TANZANIA
- Christian 45
- Muslim 35
- traditional 20

UGANDA
- Roman Catholic 33
- Protestant 33
- Muslim 16
- traditional 18

RURAL LIFE

Almost 80% of people in East Africa still live in rural areas, and for them daily life is very different. Many of them live in small villages and have farms nearby where they grow enough food to feed their families and a little extra to sell. The whole family, which may include six or seven children, are involved in the farm and often work from sunrise to sunset. Some people may find paying work on large plantation farms, such as the tea estates near Kericho in southwestern Kenya.

▲ *A fruit and vegetable market at Kakamega, Kenya. These women may have traveled a long way to sell their produce.*

Women and girls have to work especially hard in rural areas. Here three girls are pounding corn to make flour.

Rural children are lucky if they go to school. Even if they do, the schools often lack basic items such as desks, books, and paper.

In other areas they may grow crops to sell to larger farms and factories, that will then export them.

People are generally much poorer in the rural areas, living in very basic homes with no electricity or services. They have to

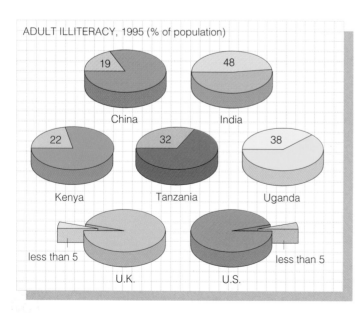

ADULT ILLITERACY, 1995 (% of population)

China 19	India 48
Kenya 22	Tanzania 32	Uganda 38
U.K. less than 5	U.S. less than 5

People may use local resources to make furniture or crafts to sell in urban markets. These men near Lake Victoria are making chairs from papyrus reeds.

EDUCATION

Education in rural areas is very poor. Children must help on the family farm or in the home. In some parts of Kenya fewer than half enroll in school, compared with a national average of 90%. Elementary education is free, but families have to find money for books, uniforms, and stationery. Many parents can only afford to send one or two of their children to school, and it is usually the girls who stay at home. This means that more than 30% of the adult population in East Africa cannot read or write. In some very rural areas, the figure may be as high as 70% among women.

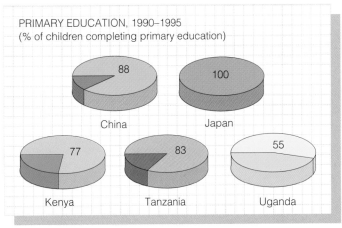

PRIMARY EDUCATION, 1990–1995
(% of children completing primary education)

88 China
100 Japan
77 Kenya
83 Tanzania
55 Uganda

spend many hours collecting wood for cooking and water for drinking. Some people make items such as cane furniture, carvings, and baskets to try to earn a little extra money, but it is a full-time job just growing enough food to feed the family.

KEY FACTS

● In Uganda's rural areas, only 42% of the population has access to health services, compared with 99% in urban areas.
● In 1994 the number of people per doctor in Uganda was 26,850 – over 60 times more people than in the U.S. or U.K.
● The average daily calorie supply in Tanzania is 2,100 (about 95% of recommended levels), while in the U.S. and U.K. it is over 3,300 (30% more than needed).

RULES AND LAWS

Kenya, Tanzania, and Uganda have existed as independent countries only since the 1960s. Until then they were European colonies, with the British controlling all three after 1918. Before that date mainland Tanzania was a German colony known as German East Africa. The British gained control after the German defeat in World War I. The territory was renamed Tanganyika, and it remained

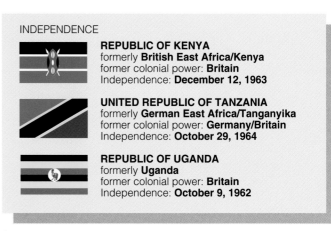

INDEPENDENCE

REPUBLIC OF KENYA
formerly **British East Africa/Kenya**
former colonial power: **Britain**
Independence: **December 12, 1963**

UNITED REPUBLIC OF TANZANIA
formerly **German East Africa/Tanganyika**
former colonial power: **Germany/Britain**
Independence: **October 29, 1964**

REPUBLIC OF UGANDA
formerly **Uganda**
former colonial power: **Britain**
Independence: **October 9, 1962**

under British control until 1961, when it peacefully gained independence under the leadership of Julius Nyerere. In 1964 Tanganyika united with the British-controlled island of Zanzibar, and the new country was named Tanzania.

Julius Nyerere believed in SOCIALISM and launched an experimental program of UJAMAA villages, where rural people would live and work collectively to develop the country's agriculture. In 1967 he expanded his socialist policy with a widespread NATIONALIZATION program proclaimed in the Arusha Declaration, a significant event in African political history. During the 1970s socialist development continued. Rural people were first persuaded and later forced to move into large collective villages. This process of "villagization," involved moving more

▲ *Julius Nyerere became the first president of independent Tanzania in 1964. He pursued a socialist system.*

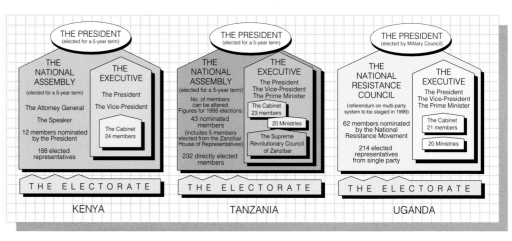

THE PRESIDENT
(elected for a 5-year term)

THE NATIONAL ASSEMBLY
(elected for a 5-year term)

The Attorney General
The Speaker
12 members nominated by the President
188 elected representatives

THE EXECUTIVE
The President
The Vice-President
The Cabinet 24 members

THE ELECTORATE

KENYA

THE PRESIDENT
(elected for a 5-year term)

THE NATIONAL ASSEMBLY
(elected for a 5-year term)
No. of members can be altered. Figures for 1995 elections.
43 nominated members
(includes 5 members elected from the Zanzibar House of Representatives)
232 directly elected members

THE EXECUTIVE
The President
The Vice-President
The Prime Minister
The Cabinet 23 members
20 Ministries
The Supreme Revolutionary Council of Zanzibar

THE ELECTORATE

TANZANIA

THE PRESIDENT
(elected by Military Council)

THE NATIONAL RESISTANCE COUNCIL
(referendum on multi-party system to be staged in 1999)
62 members nominated by the National Resistance Movement
214 elected representatives from single party

THE EXECUTIVE
The President
The Vice-President
The Prime Minister
The Cabinet 21 members
20 Ministries

THE ELECTORATE

UGANDA

than 2.5 million people into over 5,000 settlements, with the aim of increasing agricultural productivity and improving the standards of living. It is generally agreed that villagization failed, and by the 1980s Tanzania had started to move away from the socialist program.

Kenya was the scene of a violent independence struggle led by an African rebel group, the Mau Mau, who terrorized British settlers and their supporters in an attempt to drive them out of the country. Between 1952 and 1956, 100 Europeans

and around 2,000 of their African sympathizers were killed by the Mau Mau. Government forces killed about 12,000 Mau Mau rebels, mostly from the Kikuyu tribe who dominated the movement.

Many African people were held in detention centers during the troubles, and suspected leaders were arrested, including Jomo Kenyatta, who later became Kenya's first

▼ *Dignitaries, including Jomo Kenyatta, gather for Kenya's Independence Day celebrations in 1963.*

KEY FACTS

● Between 1980 and 1994, the amount of official developmental aid received by East Africa more than doubled.

● In 1994 Uganda's armed forces had 50,000 troops — more than double the number of troops it had in 1984.

● During the years of instability in Uganda, an estimated 500,000 people lost their lives, most when Idi Amin was in power.

● Kenya has 78 prisons designed to hold 21,000 prisoners, but by July 1995 they were housing nearly 50,000 inmates.

● In November 1995 Benjamin Mkapa became president of Tanzania after winning the country's first elections to be contested by different political parties.

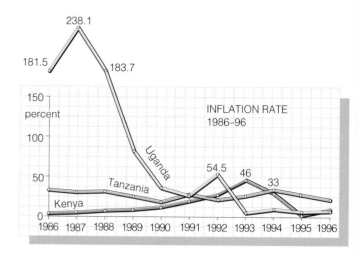

INFLATION RATE 1986–96

president. Although the Mau Mau failed in their rebellion, the British government lost confidence in its ability to control the country and promised independence to Kenya, which finally came in 1963.

As Kenya's president, Jomo Kenyatta set about building a strong, stable economy. He died in 1978 and was succeeded by Daniel arap Moi, who continued to build

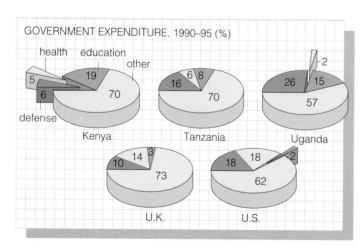

GOVERNMENT EXPENDITURE, 1990–95 (%)

▲ **Daniel arap Moi being sworn in as the new President of Kenya in 1978.**

the economy. Moi was reluctant to accept criticism of his policies and has more or less eliminated opposition parties in Kenya.

Uganda became independent in 1962 under Milton Obote. Almost immediately the country entered a period of violence and turmoil as competition erupted between the country's system of tribal kingdoms.

▲ *A stockpile of poached ivory is torched in Kenya's Nairobi National Park. President Moi has introduced tough laws to protect Kenya's wildlife from poachers.*

Obote exiled the most powerful leaders (kabakas), strengthening his control at the same time, but this led to economic collapse and allegations of corruption. In 1971 Obote's military leader, Idi Amin, staged a military coup and took control of the country.

Over the next eight years, Idi Amin conducted a reign of terror in Uganda, banning opposition parties, torturing people who spoke out against him, wiping out opposing tribal groups, and expelling the entire Asian population of around 65,000 people. In 1978 Amin's army attacked Tanzania, but Nyerere massed his troops and drove Amin back into Uganda, eventually forcing him to flee the country.

With Amin ousted and Nyerere's troops maintaining a fragile peace, Uganda set about rebuilding its tattered nation. Obote came to power again in 1980. When Tanzanian troops withdrew in 1982, political chaos and violence returned, leading to a second military coup in 1986. The new military president, Yoweri Museveni, has brought relative stability and peace to Uganda. The rebuilding of the economy and INFRASTRUCTURE provides great hope for the future of the country.

FOOD AND FARMING

CASH CROPS

Farming is the main activity in East Africa, employing more than 80% of the population. Most of the region's major commodities are based on agriculture, and for some products the region is a major world producer. For example, Uganda is the world's fifth-largest coffee producer, and Kenya is fourth in world production of tea. The islands of Pemba and Zanzibar, off the coast of Tanzania, are even more significant. They are the world's biggest producers of cloves, a spice used in cooking.

All these crops are known as "cash crops," which means they are grown mainly for

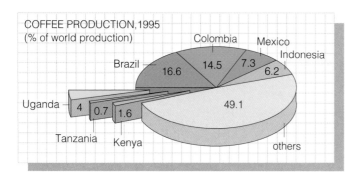

COFFEE PRODUCTION, 1995
(% of world production)

Colombia 14.5
Mexico 7.3
Indonesia 6.2
Brazil 16.6
Uganda 4
Tanzania 0.7
Kenya 1.6
others 49.1

▲ *Pemba and Zanzibar are the world's biggest producers of cloves. After they have been picked, the cloves are spread out on large mats to dry in the sun.*

selling on the world markets rather than for consumption by local people. Cash crops are normally worth more money than local crops, but there is always the risk that prices will fall because of changing world demands. For that reason it is a good idea for farmers to grow several different crops. If the price of one crop falls, there is still another to sell. Another reason for growing several crops is to reduce the impact of drought, disease, or pests, which can devastate one crop but leave another untouched.

▲ *Coffee beans are picked from bushes before being dried and processed. East Africa is one of the world's major coffee-bean producers.*

SUBSISTENCE FARMING

Although agriculture is an important industry, providing employment for thousands of people and earning valuable foreign exchange for the economy, most farmers use at least half of their land to grow food for their families or for sale in local markets. The type of crops grown varies greatly throughout the region, depending on soil, rainfall, and temperature. African farmers are very skilled and understand their local environment at least as well as the best scientists. In some cases their knowledge is much greater. By growing crops with different water needs, such as cassava

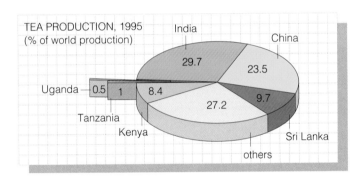

TEA PRODUCTION, 1995
(% of world production)
India 29.7
China 23.5
Sri Lanka 9.7
Kenya 27.2
Tanzania 8.4
Uganda 0.5
1
others

KEY FACTS

● In 1995–96, Uganda produced 4.1 million bags of coffee (the most for 20 years), but low prices meant earnings fell to US$ 388.9 million, down from US$ 432.6 million the previous season.
● With a total area of just 378 square miles (980 sq km), Pemba has over 3 million clove trees — more than 7,700 per square mile (3,000 per square km).
● In Tanzania about 20% of the land has over 29.5 inches (750 mm) of rain a year (the minimum needed for cultivation), but only 8% is actually cultivated.
● East Africa's agricultural labor force declined by 8% between 1960 and 1990, compared with falls of 21% in Bangladesh, 27% in Mexico, and 47% in Botswana.
● Between 1981 and 1993, food production per person fell by around 20% in Kenya and Tanzania but grew by nearly 10% in Uganda.

(which needs very little water compared with corn), they can ensure that they will have some food even if it rains very little.

Most farmers grow some crops known as "staple crops." These are items that form the basis of their diet, such as wheat and potatoes in the U.S. and U.K., or rice in much of Asia. In East Africa the staple crops are corn, millet, sorghum, cassava, and MATOKE. A matoke looks like a banana, but has a special taste and is boiled before

◀ *Kenya is a major producer of tea. Once ready, the green leaves are picked by thousands of workers and carried in large baskets to the plantation factory, where they are processed.*

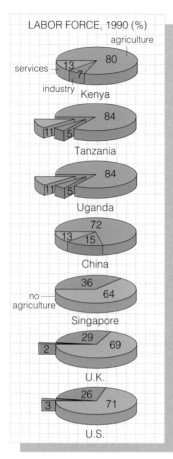

LABOR FORCE, 1990 (%)

agriculture

services — 13 | 7 | 80
industry
Kenya

84 | 11 | 5
Tanzania

84 | 11 | 5
Uganda

72 | 13 | 15
China

36 | 64
Singapore

29 | 69 | 2
U.K.

26 | 71 | 3
U.S.

no agriculture

▼ *Fishing has become a key part of the economy around Lake Victoria.*

it is eaten. It belongs to a group of plants called "plantains" that are also eaten by people in parts of South America and Asia.

In addition to staple crops, farmers also grow vegetables such as chilies, tomatoes, and beans, and various fruits including mangoes, bananas, and papaws. At first sight many fields look very disorganized, but a closer look shows how the farmer plants several different crops on the same piece of land. This is a technique known as "intercropping," which ensures a regular supply of food throughout the year as the various crops are planted and harvested at different times.

People also eat meat from chickens, sheep, and goats and use milk from cattle. Cattle are very important to African farmers. To many pastoral groups, they are seen as

a symbol of wealth. The Masai are one such group, who live mainly by herding their cattle and exchanging milk for meat and vegetables. The Masai have a traditional drink which is made of cow's milk that is mixed with fresh blood taken from a vein in the cow's neck.

FISHING

People living around Lake Victoria and other freshwater lakes supplement their diet with fish. In recent years fishing has increased dramatically and is now an important part of the local economy. Traditionally the main fish caught in Lake Victoria were tilapia, similar to carp, and a small sardinelike fish called omena. However, during the 1950s the British introduced a fish called the Nile perch,

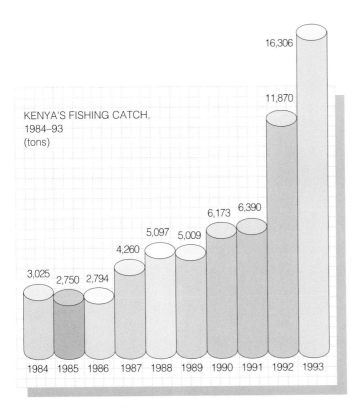

KENYA'S FISHING CATCH,
1984–93
(tons)

16,306

11,870

6,390

6,173

5,097 5,009

4,260

3,025 2,750 2,794

1984 1985 1986 1987 1988 1989 1990 1991 1992 1993

which has permanently changed the nature of the lake.

The Nile perch, which can weigh as much as a small adult, is an aggressive predator that eats many other fish in Lake Victoria. It was introduced for eating and today accounts for a large proportion of the fish catch. The Nile perch is popular outside Africa, and there are several factories that package it to sell in European and Israeli supermarkets.

In the past few years, increased fishing activity on Lake Victoria has meant that many fish are caught before they reach breeding age, so there is a risk that the number of catches will begin to fall in the near future. There is also a problem with a weed called the water hyacinth that has spread over large sections of the lake,

◀ *The Nile perch is an introduced species that has boosted the local economy, but it has also eaten many of the native freshwater species.*

KEY FACTS

● The Masai graze more than 100,000 cattle in Tanzania's Ngorongoro Crater, which they share with approximately 30,000 wild animals.

● Kenya's fishing catch increased by over 500% between 1984 and 1993, reaching a total of 16,306 tons.

● In 1995, Kenya's horticulture industry earned 10.6 billion Kenyan shillings (US$ 207 million) – up from 3.2 billion in 1990.

● Together with Zambia and Zimbabwe, Kenya, Tanzania, and Uganda produce over 900 million roses a year.

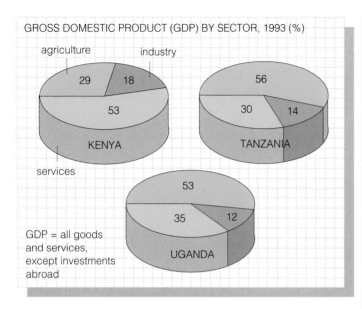

GROSS DOMESTIC PRODUCT (GDP) BY SECTOR, 1993 (%)

agriculture   industry

29   18

53

KENYA

services

56

30   14

TANZANIA

53

35   12

UGANDA

GDP = all goods
and services,
except investments
abroad

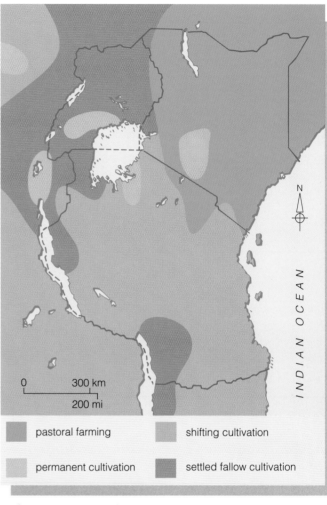

0   300 km
    200 mi

pastoral farming   shifting cultivation

permanent cultivation   settled fallow cultivation

INDIAN OCEAN

N

making it difficult for fishermen to pull up
their nets and get their boats to shore.

HORTICULTURE

The most recent development in the region's
farming was the growth of the horticultural
industry during the 1980s. This involves the
production of fresh fruit, vegetables, and
cut flowers for sale in European, Asian, and

◀ *These women
in Zanzibar are
grinding millet
between two
heavy stones to
crush the grain
into a flour. The
flour is then used
to make a type of
porridge that is
one of the staple
foods in East
Africa.*

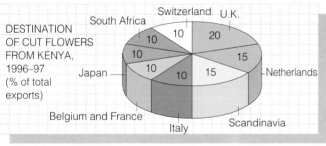

DESTINATION
OF CUT FLOWERS
FROM KENYA,
1996–97
(% of total
exports)

South Africa
Switzerland   U.K.
10   10   20
10   15
Japan   10   10   15   Netherlands
Belgium and France
Italy   Scandinavia

▲ *Flowers are an important part of*
Kenya's flourishing horticulture industry.
They are grown in specially controlled
greenhouses – such as here, in Thika –
and then exported all over the world.

Middle Eastern markets. Products include
mangoes, melons, green beans, avocados,
and flowers such as roses, chrysanthemums,
and lilies.

The industry employs thousands of
people and is growing very quickly to
satisfy European demand for fresh food
and flowers throughout the year. Smaller
farmers have not yet benefited much from
this new market because they cannot
compete with the big producers. In Kenya
small farmers are beginning to organize
themselves into cooperative groups so that
they can compete effectively, but it is not
yet clear how well this type of farming
production will work in East Africa.

TRADE AND INDUSTRY

East Africa's industrial sector is very small compared with African economies such as South Africa, Zimbabwe, and Nigeria. There are petroleum refineries at Mombasa, Kenya, while Uganda and Kenya have some metal-processing and car plants, but they employ few people and contribute relatively little to the economy.

Tourism is an important industry throughout the region. In Kenya, where it is most developed, it is one of the biggest earners of foreign exchange. Tourists are attracted by the region's fantastic landscape, abundant wildlife, and friendly people. Tanzania has the best opportunity to develop its tourist industry because of its enormous national parks. The Selous Game Reserve in the south of the country is the largest in the world, covering an area of 19,300 square miles (50,000 sq km) — nearly twice the size of neighboring Rwanda and bigger than Switzerland.

One rapidly growing industry is the processing of agricultural products such as tea, coffee, vegetables, and fruit. As the demand for these goods increases on the world markets, this sector should continue to expand. It is an important industry, largely because it is more profitable for countries to process their own goods than export them in a raw state.

East Africa's main trading partners are European, with the U.K., Germany, and Spain being particularly important. Other key partners include Japan and India.

Kenya, Tanzania, and Uganda are striving to establish a regional cooperation for trade, to be called East African Cooperation (EAC).

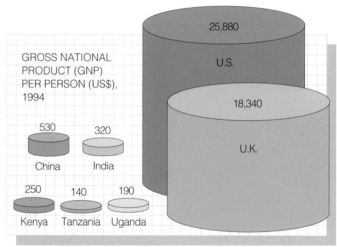

GROSS NATIONAL PRODUCT (GNP) PER PERSON (US$), 1994

25,880 U.S.

18,340 U.K.

530 China

320 India

250 Kenya

140 Tanzania

190 Uganda

◀ *Tourism is very important in East Africa, creating jobs and an income for many local people. Here in Masai Mara, tourists are watching the lions — or is it the other way around?*

◀ *Processing food, such as pineapples, has become an important industry in East Africa.*

▼ *Here, German cars are being built by workers at a plant in Thika, Kenya.*

This would be similar to the European Union (EU) or the North American Free Trade Agreement (NAFTA), allowing for special trading arrangements between the member countries, such as the lifting of import and export duties.

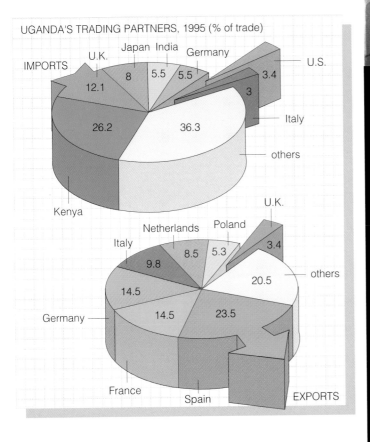

UGANDA'S TRADING PARTNERS, 1995 (% of trade)

IMPORTS

U.K. 12.1
Japan 8
India 5.5
Germany 5.5
U.S. 3.4
Italy 3
others 36.3
Kenya 26.2

EXPORTS

U.K. 3.4
Poland 5.3
Netherlands 8.5
Italy 9.8
Germany 14.5
France 14.5
Spain 23.5
others 20.5

KEY FACTS

● In the U.S. GROSS NATIONAL PRODUCT per person is around 100 times greater than Kenya's and almost 185 times greater than Tanzania's.
● The number of visitors to Kenya rose from 362,000 in 1980 to 676,000 in 1994, but fell below 500,000 in 1996. Most came from Germany and the U.K.
● In Kenya earnings from processing horticultural produce rose dramatically, from 1.52 billion Kenyan shillings in 1990 to 3.33 billion in 1994 (about US$ 64 million).

TRANSPORTATION

East Africa's transportation system is not at all developed compared with those of Europe or North America, but for Africa it is relatively good. Paved roads connect the main centers of activity, but many are in poor condition. Few people own cars, so most use buses or the brightly colored minibuses known as matatus to travel by road.

The main regional railroad was built by the British and runs from Mombasa to Kasese, near Uganda's border with Congo. Nairobi, now the region's main city, began life as a storage depot for the railroad's construction workers. Tanzania has a separate rail network that was built by the Germans and extended by the British. It spreads westward from Dar es Salaam in a fan shape, with one line, built by the Chinese in the 1960s, continuing into Zambia. Travel by rail is very slow, and there often is only one train a day between main centers.

Lake Victoria is important for the region's transportation system. Ferries operate both local and international routes. Most are open-decked and very crowded, carrying everything from cars and buses to people

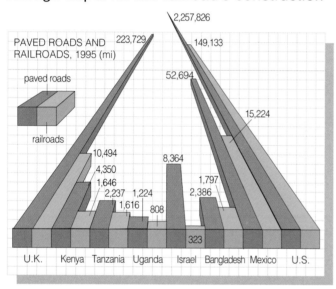

PAVED ROADS AND RAILROADS, 1995 (mi)

paved roads

railroads

2,257,826
223,729
149,133
52,694
15,224
10,494
4,350
1,646
2,237 1,224
1,616 808
8,364
1,797
2,386
323

U.K.   Kenya Tanzania Uganda Israel Bangladesh Mexico U.S.

KEY FACTS

● In 1994 Kenya had about 5 cars per 1,000 people, while Tanzania and Uganda had less than 2 per 1,000. The United States had 589 per 1,000.

● The volume of freight passing through Mombasa's port to neighboring countries rose from 579,863 tons in 1991 to 1,330,975 tons in 1995.

● Kenya has seen the region's biggest expansion in air traffic: from 393,000 passengers in 1980 to more than 750,000 by 1994.

◀ *Open-decked ferries operating on Lake Victoria are an important form of transportation for trade and travel between all three East African countries.*

taking their goats or chickens to market.

Nairobi is a major air TRANSPORTATION-HUB, and the volume of traffic has been increasing. There are several flights a day between the region's main cities, and several new airports are being planned to accommodate the increase in international traffic.

The Indian Ocean ports of Mombasa and Dar es Salaam are two of the busiest in Africa. They are very important for trade with Europe, the Middle East, and India. They serve many of Africa's landlocked states, with freight being transferred by road or railroad.

However, for many people in the region, walking or cycling is the main means of travel. It is not unusual for people to walk more than 15 miles (24 km) to reach a market or place of work.

▲ *Air travel is the easiest way to cover the large distances between the region's main centers, or to reach parks and reserves such as the Masai Mara.*

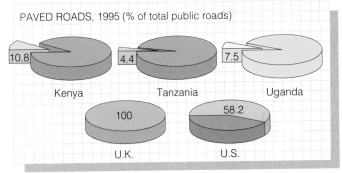

PAVED ROADS, 1995 (% of total public roads)

10.8	4.4	7.5
Kenya	Tanzania	Uganda
100	58.2	
U.K.	U.S.	

▶ *Crowded buses cover most of the main routes between towns.*

THE ENVIRONMENT

The region has a rich and varied natural environment. The rain forests of western Uganda are the last in East Africa and are home to about 300 mountain gorillas — about half the total world population of this highly endangered species. The savanna plains that cover southern Kenya and most of Tanzania contain a fantastic variety of large mammal wildlife, including elephants, giraffes, zebras, lions, wildebeests, and many types of antelope. This area is almost uninhabited by humans apart from a few pastoral communities. The great lakes of the region, such as Lakes Victoria, Turkana, and Tanganyika, provide another important natural environment, while the soda lakes of the Rift Valley have a very rare ecology all their own.

East Africa has its share of environmental problems. Its rapidly growing population has created a great deal of pressure on the environment. In some areas there is now great cause for concern. The region's main problems are water shortages, deforestation, soil erosion, and desertificaton. These

◄ Savanna areas are sparsely populated by pastoral people. They regularly move their grazing livestock to avoid damaging the environment.

difficulties are frequently related so that one leads to another or increases the chances of a new one occurring.

Traffic and waste pollution are problems in urban areas. In some of the shantytowns they present a serious health hazard. The shortage of safe water and adequate sanitation facilities is one of the region's biggest problems, especially in overcrowded city slums. People are often forced to drink water that may have been used for washing, cleaning clothes, and watering livestock. Many of the region's major diseases, such as hepatitis, typhoid, dysentery, and diarrhea, are transmitted by using dirty water, so infection rates are often very high

▼ Not all of East Africa's environmental problems are caused by people. Heavy storms can cause massive soil erosion, or "gullying."

KEY FACTS

● In 1994 nationally protected areas covered 14.7% of Tanzania's total land, 8.1% of Uganda's, and 6% of Kenya's.

● In the 1960s the Masai protested at the loss of their grazing lands by killing rhinos and elephants in Amboseli National Park, southern Kenya.

● Since Kenya introduced an ivory ban in 1989, the number of elephants poached has fallen from 5,000 a year to 50 or 60. The elephant population also has increased by about 1,000 every year.

that the environment is important for the tourist industry and have set up more than 97 nationally protected areas to preserve the region's landscapes and wildlife. Some 53,670 square miles (139,000 sq km) of Tanzania's total area are set aside as protected areas, including the Selous Game Reserve, the largest reserve in the world. In Kenya's Nakuru National Park, black rhinos are heavily protected behind electric fences patrolled by armed guards. This is because poaching reduced Kenya's rhino population from about 20,000 in 1970 to less than 500 by the late 1980s. On the other hand, this type of protection can disrupt local people's lives, sometimes causing conflict. The Masai, for example, who traditionally used

in crowded slum areas. Many rural areas also lack safe water and sanitation facilities, so people have to use the nearest stream, river, or lake to meet their requirements.

The East African people are very aware of their environment because so many of them rely on the land, and its wildlife for their livelihood. Governments also know

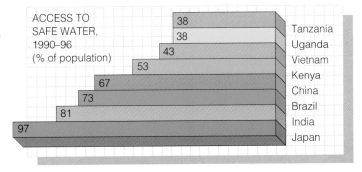

ACCESS TO SAFE WATER, 1990–96 (% of population)

38	Tanzania
38	Uganda
43	Vietnam
53	Kenya
67	China
73	Brazil
81	India
97	Japan

▶ *Lack of safe water and sanitation facilities means that urban slums – such as this one in Kampala, Uganda – are often plagued with health problems. One major hazard is malaria. It is transmitted by mosquitoes, which breed in shallow pools and streams.*

park lands for collecting food, grazing livestock, and hunting game, have been severely affected by the designation of many national parks in Kenya.

In many parts of East Africa, local people work together with the government or overseas agencies on local small-scale programs to protect the environment. Projects include planting trees to replace those cut down for firewood. The roots of these new trees also bind the soil, so reducing soil erosion, while planting fruit trees can provide food for local people to eat or to sell. Other tree species can

▼ *The region's rhino population is protected inside special reserves. This rhino is near Ngorongoro Crater, Tanzania.*

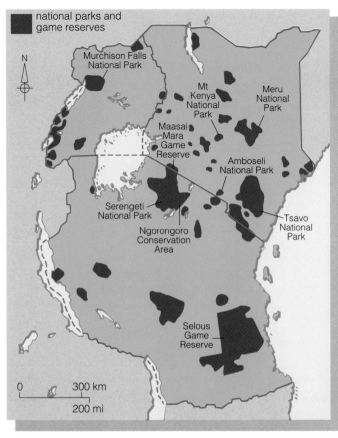

national parks and game reserves

Murchison Falls National Park

Mt Kenya National Park

Meru National Park

Maasai Mara Game Reserve

Amboseli National Park

Serengeti National Park

Ngorongoro Conservation Area

Tsavo National Park

Selous Game Reserve

N

0   300 km

200 mi

provide fodder for animals, firewood, and building materials. It can also act as a fertilizer, depending on the farmers' needs. This multiple use of trees is known as "agroforestry," a combination of agriculture and forestry, and is considered very important for the future of East Africa's environment.

Other local projects, such as the one in Machakos District, near Nairobi, Kenya, include TERRACING on slopes to prevent soil erosion, building small dams in order to catch and store rainwater, and improved crop management.

▶ *In dry rural areas such as northern Kenya, people may have to dig deep holes to reach water underground.*

◀ *Tree nurseries are often organized by local people with money from the government or other agencies. Later, the trees will be planted elsewhere to protect the soil and to provide firewood, fruit, and other resources. It is especially common for women's groups to be involved in these projects – such as this one in Meru, Kenya.*

43

THE FUTURE

◀ *New buildings such as this one in Nairobi are emerging in many cities, as the region's new stability attracts business and investment from throughout the world.*

East Africa is entering a period of new challenges and fresh opportunities. The plans for a new East African Cooperation will reinforce the area's political and economic stability and allow it to compete with the southern African states that have emerged as Africa's major economic region since the mid-1990s. Kenya's important tourist industry has already lost up to 20% of its visitors to South Africa and Zimbabwe, and competition is likely to increase in the agricultural sector, too. Horticultural production has great potential to strengthen the East African economies, especially since land is plentiful. It can also lead to other industries (such as processing and packaging) that increase export income and provide more jobs.

Any future developments in East Africa must be able to support the rapidly growing population for many years without harming the environment on which so many people rely. Projects such as tree nurseries, soil protection, and water management must be encouraged through rural development projects that also provide basic services such as education and health. These projects make rural living more attractive and encourage people to remain in the villages, rather than migrate to already overcrowded urban areas.

East Africa's most important challenges for the future are to maintain peace and stability, to promote regional cooperation, and to meet the basic needs of its people. Achieving these aims will allow the population to develop the skills necessary to take East Africa into the 21st century.

KEY FACTS

● In 1996 Kenya's government and the World Bank launched a US$ 165 million program to upgrade and maintain the country's road network.

● During 1996 new gold reserves were discovered around the southern shores of Lake Victoria in Tanzania. Production is expected to start in 1999.

● The East African Cooperation (EAC) is due to expand into a Common Market for East and South Africa (COMESA) by the year 2000.

▲ *Cooperative projects such as this soil-and-water management project in Kenya, are important for maintaining rural development.*

▶ *More and more tourists are looking for adventurous vacations in remote areas. This is a potential key industry for East Africa.*

FURTHER INFORMATION

● KENYAN TOURIST OFFICE
424 Madison Ave.
New York, NY 10017
Provides posters, leaflets and general information on Kenya.
● TANZANIAN TOURIST OFFICE
205 East 42nd St., 8th Floor
New York, NY 10017
Provides general information on Tanzania.
● UGANDAN HIGH COMMISSION
231 Coburg St.
Ottawa, Ontario
Canada
Provides general information on Uganda.

BOOKS ABOUT EAST AFRICA
● Blauer, Ettagale and Jason Laure. *Tanzania.* Children's Press, 1994
● Lisicky, Paul. *Uganda.* Chelsea House, 1988
● Pateman, Robert. *Kenya.* Marshall Cavendish, 1994
● Regan, Colm and Peter Cremin. *Africa.* Raintree Steck-Vaughn, 1997
● Stein, R. Conrad. *Kenya.* Childrens Press, 1985
● Wepman, Dennis. *Jomo Keyatta.* Chelsea House, 1985

GLOSSARY

CASH CROPS
Crops that are grown mainly for sale in overseas markets but can also be sold in local markets.

DESERTIFICATION
The process whereby a piece of land becomes barren and infertile. It can be caused by deforestation, overcultivation, and soil erosion. It is very difficult to reverse.

GEOLOGICAL FAULT
A line of weakness in the Earth's crust. It is caused by violent movement deep inside the Earth. Volcanoes and earthquakes are often associated with these areas.

GROSS NATIONAL PRODUCT (GNP)
The total value of all the goods and services produced by a country in a year.

INDEPENDENCE
The transfer of power from a foreign government to one set up by local people, who are then able to control their own affairs.

INFRASTRUCTURE
A network for transmitting and transporting basic things such as water, electricity, information, or vehicles. Examples are sewer pipes and highways.

MATATUS
Minibuses used in East Africa to transport people and their goods. They are often brightly colored, and the driver sometimes plays loud music.

MATOKE
A somewhat spicy banana eaten as a staple food in Uganda. A matoke (or plantain, as it is known elsewhere) is peeled and boiled before being eaten.

MINIMUM WAGE JOBS
Although usually not recognized officially, this part of the economy involves people selling various goods or offering different services in casual settings such as in the streets or in markets.

NATIONALIZATION
The process of government taking control of major industries, transportation networks, and financial institutions. This is the opposite of privatization and is normally associated with socialist and communist governments.

NOMADIC
A lifestyle where people move from place to place. Livestock herders often are nomadic, moving with their animals in search of pasture and water.

PASTORALISTS
People who make their living by herding animals. The Masai are an example of a pastoral community.

SAVANNA
A tropical vegetation consisting of grasses, shrubs, and scattered trees. It is typically dry for most of the year but bursts into life when the first rains arrive.

SEMIARID
Describes a halfway zone between savanna grassland and desert. Vegetation is typically sparse due to lack of rainfall.

SOCIALISM
A system of government based on the idea that resources and profits are shared rather than concentrated in the hands of certain individuals or small groups.

SODA LAKE
Also known as alkali lake, contains concentrations of salt compounds. Usually occurs in desert areas and has no outlets.

TERRACING
Cutting strips of farmland into the side of a hill, forming a pattern of "steps." This practice reduces soil erosion.

TRANSPORTATION-HUB
The meeting or crossover point of major roads, railroads, sea and air routes. These usually are in large cities such as Dar es Salaam, Nairobi, London, New York, and Tokyo.

UJAMAA
A Swahili word meaning "familyhood." In Tanzania it refers to village settlements where people live and work together on agricultural projects.

INDEX

© Macdonald Young Books
1998